W9-AWZ-207

LET'S READ
ABOUT
Animals

Sea Turtles

by Kathleen Pohl

Reading consultant: Susan Nations, M.Ed.,
author/literacy coach/consultant
in literacy development

WEEKLY READER®
PUBLISHING

Please visit our web site at: www.garethstevens.com
For a free color catalog describing our list of high-quality books,
call 1-800-542-2595 (USA) or 1-800-387-3178 (Canada).
Our fax: 877-542-2596.

Library of Congress Cataloging-in-Publication Data

Pohl, Kathleen.
    Sea turtles / by Kathleen Pohl.
        p. cm. — (Let's read about animals)
    Includes bibliographical references and index.
    ISBN-13: 978-0-8368-7820-2 (lib. bdg.)
    ISBN-13: 978-0-8368-7827-1 (softcover)
    1. Sea turtles—Juvenile literature. I. Title.
QL666.C536.P64   2007
    597.92—dc22   2006030870

This edition first published in 2007 by
Weekly Reader® Books
An Imprint of Gareth Stevens Publishing
1 Reader's Digest Road
Pleasantville, NY 10570-7000 USA

Copyright © 2007 by Weekly Reader® Early Learning Library

Editor: Dorothy L. Gibbs
Art Direction: Tammy West
Cover design and page layout: Kami Strunsee
Picture research: Diane Laska-Swanke

Picture credits: Cover, title © Doug Perrine/naturepl.com; pp. 5, 7, 11 © Doug Perrine/
Auscape; p. 9 © Tobias Bernhard-OSF/Auscape; pp. 13, 21 © Jürgen Freund/Auscape;
pp. 14-15 Kami Strunsee/© Weekly Reader® Early Learning Library; p. 17 © Jean-Paul Ferrero/
Auscape; p. 19 © Dr. David Wachenfeld/Auscape

All rights reserved. No part of this book may be reproduced, stored in a retrieval system,
or transmitted in any form or by any means, electronic, mechanical, photocopying,
recording, or otherwise, without the prior written permission of the copyright holder.

Printed in the United States of America

2 3 4 5 6 7 8 9 10 10 09 08

Note to Educators and Parents

Reading is such an exciting adventure for young children! They are beginning to integrate their oral language skills with written language. To encourage children along the path to early literacy, books must be colorful, engaging, and interesting; they should invite the young reader to explore both the print and the pictures.

The *Let's Read About Animals* series is designed to help children read and learn about the special characteristics and behaviors of the intriguing featured animals. Each book is an informative nonfiction companion to one of the colorful and charming fiction books in the *Animal Storybooks* series.

Each book in the *Let's Read About Animals* series is specially designed to support the young reader in the reading process. The familiar topics are appealing to young children and invite them to read — and reread — again and again. The full-color photographs and enhanced text further support the student during the reading process.

In addition to serving as wonderful picture books in schools, libraries, homes, and other places where children learn to love reading, these books are specifically intended to be read within an instructional guided reading group. This small group setting allows beginning readers to work with a fluent adult model as they make meaning from the text. After children develop fluency with the text and content, the books can be read independently. Children and adults alike will find these books supportive, engaging, and fun!

— Susan Nations, M.Ed., author/literacy coach/
consultant in literacy development

You will not see a turtle like this one in a pond! **Sea turtles** are much bigger than pond turtles.

green turtle

Sea turtles live in **oceans**.

They are very good swimmers.

hawksbill turtle

They have **flippers** to help them swim. Sea turtles move their flippers like oars on a boat.

flipper

Most sea turtles eat meat. They catch fish and snails with their strong **beaks**.

loggerhead turtle

beak

A sea turtle has a hard **shell**. Its shell keeps the turtle safe from enemies.

shell

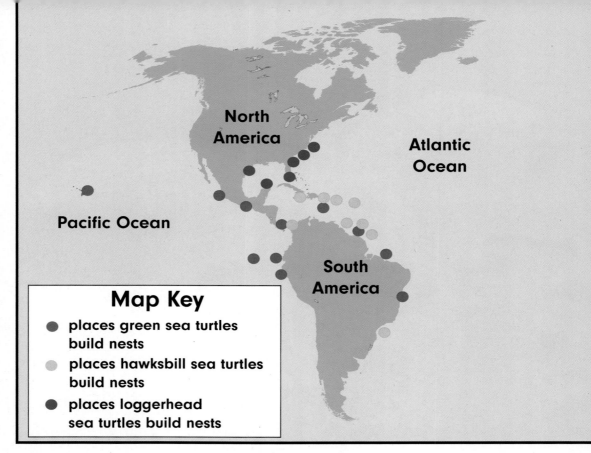

Map Key
- places green sea turtles build nests
- places hawksbill sea turtles build nests
- places loggerhead sea turtles build nests

North America

Atlantic Ocean

Pacific Ocean

South America

This map shows many places in the world where sea turtles build their **nests**.

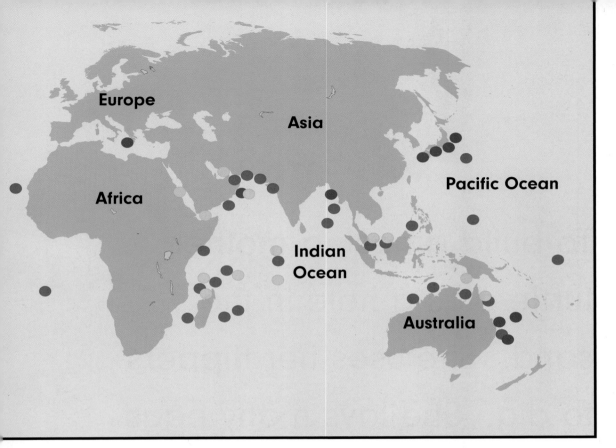

A sea turtle always goes back
to the same **beach** to build a
nest and to lay eggs.

To build a nest, a mother turtle digs a hole in the sand. She uses her flippers to dig. She lays many eggs in the hole.

eggs

The mother turtle covers the eggs with sand. Then she crawls back to the sea.

Baby turtles have many enemies on land. They must hurry to the sea to grow up. Good luck, baby turtles!

Glossary

beach — the sandy area along a seacoast

beaks — the hard outer mouthparts of turtles or birds

enemies — animals that try to harm other animals

flippers — the strong legs or feet of a sea turtle, which are used for swimming

nests — places where mother turtles and other female animals lay their eggs

oceans — the large bodies of saltwater in the world, also called seas

sea turtles — large turtles that live in the sea and have flippers for feet

shell — the hard outer covering on the body of a turtle that helps keep the turtle safe from enemies